MONWEALTH · GODFATHER · SCOTCH

UCK · MISSISSIPPI MIST · ALABAMA

OHN COLLIN   TAN

G · TRADITI   YLE

STY NAIL · OLD-FASHIONED · SAZERAC

HISKEY SOUR · NEW YORKER · BELMONT

BOBBY BURNS · CANADIAN COCKTAIL

GHT · IRISH SHILLELAGH · KENTUCKY

RÉ · SOUL KISS · LOUISVILLE STINGER

GER · EVERYBODY'S IRISH · SHAMROCK

CHILL DOWNS COOLER · MAMIE TAYLOR

· POIRE WILLIAMS FIZZ · CASANOVA

D0014524

Mini Bar *Whiskey*

Mini Bar **Whiskey**

by MITTIE HELLMICH

photographs by Laura Stojanovic

CHRONICLE BOOKS
SAN FRANCISCO

A huge thanks to the fabulously creative project manager Mary Wruck for her savvy attention to detail, and the meticulous copyeditor Jonathan Kaufman. And a special thanks to Hudson Pierce-Rhoads, Geoffrey Rhoads, and Rick Van Oel. —MH

Library of Congress Cataloging-in-Publication Data available.

ISBN 10: 0-8118-5422-1

ISBN 13: 978-0-8118-5422-1

Manufactured in China.

Prop styling by Barbara Fierros
Food styling by William Smith
Designed by Hallie Overman, Brooklyn NY

From Laura: Many thanks to Amanda & Jimmy for letting me bring a week of chaos into their house.

Distributed in Canada by Raincoast Books
9050 Shaughnessy Street
Vancouver, BC V6P 6E5

10 9 8 7 6 5 4 3 2 1

Chronicle Books LLC
85 Second Street
San Francisco, California 94105

www.chroniclebooks.com

Table of Contents

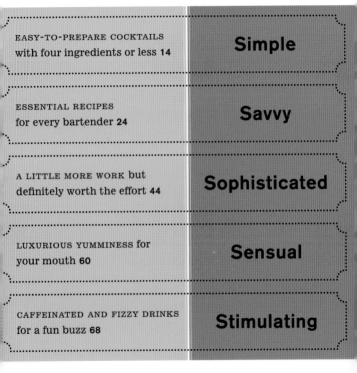

Introduction

WHEN THE SUBJECT OF WHISKEY COMES UP, no one can escape
the images it conjures of the misty green hills of Ireland,
Scottish peat bogs, the Kentucky Derby, or stuffed club
chairs and the scent of cigars. Whiskey is a spirit with multiple personalities and a rich lineage, all infused into a glass
of amber liquid that imparts a glowing warmth.

The nuanced differences among whiskeys—blended versus
straight whiskeys, or the varied production methods used
to produce them—are so numerous and complex it is impos-
sible to do them justice in this small volume. Nonetheless,
knowing a little about the basics will give you a snapshot
understanding of which whiskeys are appropriate for sipping
or mixing, as well as an excuse to indulge in adventuresome
testing. Perhaps one of the whiskeys you taste will lead you
down the obsessive road of whiskey connoisseurship.

THE HISTORY OF WHISKEY

Now, as any Irishman will tell you, Ireland is the birth-
place of whiskey distillation. Monks on the Emerald Isle are
said to have been distilling *uisege baugh*, Gaelic for "water
of life," as far back as the twelfth century. But the ancient
Gaelic Scots also had a similar word, *uisge beatha*, also
meaning "water of life," so there's a bit of contention there
over who's on first. One thing's for sure: Both Ireland and
Scotland are renowned for their whiskeys.

Irish whiskey is made from a blend of unmalted and malted
barley that is fermented and roasted over coal or gas in

closed kilns, then sent through pot stills and stored in wooden casks. The process yields a clear barley flavor and smoothness. The Irish mostly produce blended whiskeys, made from three styles of whiskey. Only a few single-malt Irish whiskeys are available.

Scotch whisky is defined by its smoky flavor, which comes from malted barley that is dried over peat fires. The distillate is barrel aged anywhere from ten to eighteen years, or even longer. When you savor a sip of scotch, they say you are experiencing all the characteristics of that particular area of Scotland. From the heathered Highlands to the sea-sprayed island of Islay, single malts are all distinctly different, taking your palate on a virtual tour of the many regions.

In the United States, our native spirits hold their own. Americans produce fine whiskeys such as bourbon, rye, and Tennessee sour mash. In fact, U.S. history is steeped in the stuff. The Whiskey Rebellion of 1794, fought over taxation (of course), was tamped down by President George Washington. Ironically, he was an aficionado of the amber liquid and had a private bourbon stash made at Mount Vernon. Abraham Lincoln shared Washington's passion, and the six-teenth president's liquid interests led to his involvement in a distillery. American whiskeys have evolved from the cow-boys' favorite bug juice and the Indians' firewater of choice to enjoy an illustrious fan base that included infamously fueling the misbehavior of the Rat Pack in the 1950s.

Our romance with Mint Juleps and the Kentucky Derby started with the all-American whiskey named after the area in which it was first made: Bourbon County, Kentucky. For a whiskey to be called *bourbon*, it must come from Kentucky and be made from at least 51 percent corn. The best bourbons come from producers of "single-barrel" or "small-batch" bourbons. They are milder and sweeter than scotch but are equally regarded by connoisseurs as great sipping whiskeys.

DISTILLING THE SPIRIT

In the most basic terms, whiskey is made from a fermented mash of corn, rye, oats, wheat, or barley. The type of grain used in the mash determines the taste and character of the resulting whiskey. Methods of production vary from traditional pot stills to more modern column stills, but all whiskeys are aged in barrels (or casks). The type of wood, size of the barrel, and length of time aged all factor into the liquor's distinctive color, aroma, and taste.

There is an art to creating blended whiskeys, which are a combination of grain whiskeys from many different distilleries. These versatile and popular lighter-bodied spirits are typically cheaper and are perfect for mixed drinks. The best high-end blends, which combine a variety of superior straight whiskeys, are complex, smooth, and sippable. The Canadians produce exceptionally smooth blended whiskies reminiscent of the spicy, bittersweet flavor of a rye yet with the vanilla sweetness of bourbon.

Finally, to answer those pesky questions concerning the missing e in whisky, it's quite simple: The Irish and Americans spell it whiskey, whereas the Scots and Canadians follow the British spelling, omitting the "e."

In whiskey mixology, there are a few general rules to keep in mind: With the exception of a few cocktails, a refined single-malt scotch or small-batch bourbon in a mixed drink gets pointlessly lost, so save your high-end whiskeys for sipping neat. Good-quality blended whiskeys can be enjoyed in mixed drinks such as a Manhattan (the whiskey lover's Martini) or over ice with a splash of club soda. Strong straight whiskeys such as rye (similar to bourbon, but not as refined) and Tennessee sour mash (similar to bourbon but sweeter) are also traditionally used in mixed drinks.

The different types of whiskeys are so divergent in taste, it brings me to whiskey mixology rule number two: The types of whiskey called for in many of the drinks in this book are based on the classic recipes—an Irish whiskey for a Blarney Stone, say, or a bourbon for a Mint Julep. It is not the classic drink if made with some other whiskey, which will change the taste considerably. Some drinks can accommodate your personal preference, such as a Whiskey Sour or classics such as the Manhattan that have changed over time as tastes have shifted.

Now that you have attained whiskey enlightenment, you are ready to dive into this little book. It may just be the tip of the misting Isle iceberg, but it's a comprehensive compilation, with a spectrum of fine-tuned classics and well-crafted contemporary cocktails for you to explore.

Cheers!

Glassware, Tools, and Terminology

Glassware plays an important role in the much-ritualized cocktail experience. A well-chilled vessel visually entices us with the promise of refreshment, with the right glass adding elegance to even the simplest drink. Glasses come in an endless variety of designs, styles, and colors, but when it comes to setting up your home bar, your repertoire of glassware doesn't have to be extensive to be stylishly appropriate and proficiently functional. A few basic styles—cocktail glasses, highball glasses, old-fashioned and double old-fashioned glasses, champagne flutes, and wineglasses—will see you beautifully through a multitude of drinks.

ESSENTIAL BAR TOOLS

Whether you have a swank bar setup in your favorite enter-taining room or an area set aside in the kitchen, you don't need all the high-tech gadgets and gizmos to put together a well-functioning home bar. All you need are the essential bar tools to see you through just about any mixological occasion. You may already have the typical kitchen tools you need: a sharp paring knife for cutting fruit and garnishes, a cutting board for cutting fruit, a bar towel, a good corkscrew and bottle opener, and measuring spoons and cups. To these you will want to add a few of the basic bar tools: a blender with a high-caliber motor, a citrus juicer, a cocktail shaker or a mixing pitcher and stirring rod, a bar spoon, a jigger, an ice bucket and tongs, and, of course, a few cocktail picks and swizzle sticks.

To dash, muddle, top, or float: That is the question. When you want clarification on what exactly that all means or what it means to have a drink served up, neat, straight, or on the rocks, this miniglossary of frequently used bar terms will assist you in navigating bar talk.

· Chaser · The beverage you drink immediately after you have downed anything alcoholic, usually a shot. Typical chasers are beer, club soda, and juice.

· Dash · Either a shake from a bitters bottle or the equivalent of approximately ⅛ teaspoon.

· Dry · A term meaning "not sweet," used either in reference to some wines or to describe nonsweet spirits or cocktails, such as the Dry Martini, which uses dry vermouth rather than sweet vermouth.

· Float · This describes the technique of slowly pouring a small amount of spirit (usually a liqueur or cream) over the surface of a drink so that it floats, or sits atop another liquid without mixing. The customary technique is to slowly pour the liquid over the back of a spoon.

· Highball · The main characteristics of a highball drink are that it has two ingredients—one spirit and one mixer, usually carbonated, poured into a tall, narrow glass filled with ice (the shape of the glass helps to contain the carbonation)—and that it can be mixed very quickly.

· Lowball · A lowball is any drink served with ice in a short glass such as an old-fashioned glass.

· Muddle · A technique that involves using a small wooden "muddler" or spoon to mash fruits or herbs in the bottom of the glass, usually together with bitters or sugar, to release their aromatic flavors.

· Neat · Describes a single spirit or liqueur served in a glass "straight up"—enjoyed on its own, unchilled, and without ice, water, or any other ingredients.

· Neutral Spirit · A spirit distilled from grain to produce a virtually tasteless, colorless alcohol that is 95.5 percent ABV (alcohol by volume) and is used as a base for spirits such as vodka or gin or for blending with straight whiskeys or other spirits and liqueurs.

· On the Rocks · A term used to describe any liquor or mixed drink served over ice—the "rocks" being ice cubes— as opposed to a drink served "up" (without ice).

· Perfect · A term used to describe specific cocktails that contain equal parts dry and sweet vermouth, as in a Perfect Manhattan or Perfect Martini.

· Pousse-Café · Literally translated as the "coffee-pusher" (and pronounced poos-caf-FAY), this after-dinner drink layers colorful strata of liqueurs, syrups, spirits, and creams in a stemmed glass. The multiple layers—as many as seven—are artfully floated one on top of another so that each stratum remains separate. The heaviest liquid goes in first, the lightest is added last.

· Proof · A legal measurement of the alcoholic strength of a spirit. In the United States, proof is calculated thusly:

1 degree of proof equals 0.5 percent ABV (alcohol by volume). Therefore, a spirit labeled "80 proof" is 40 percent ABV, a 100-proof spirit is 50 percent ABV, and so on.

· Splash · A small amount that can fall anywhere between a dash and about an ounce, depending on who's doing the splashing.

· Straight · This term describes a spirit served without any other liquor or mixers, either poured into a chilled glass or over ice, occasionally with the addition of a splash of club soda or water.

· Top or Top Off · A term used by bartenders to describe the act of pouring the last ingredient into a drink, usually club soda or ginger ale, filling to the top of the glass. Also used to describe filling a beer mug from a tap.

· Up · Describes a drink served without ice in a cocktail glass. Usually the drink is shaken in a cocktail shaker and strained "up" into a chilled cocktail glass, as opposed to "on the rocks," which means served over ice.

simple

· Easy-to-prepare cocktails with four ingredients or less ·

Kentucky Colonel

BÉNÉDICTINE IS A COGNAC-BASED HERBAL LIQUEUR from Normandy, France, that is named after the Benedictine monks of the Abbey of Fécamp. Those guys really knew what to do with botanicals—seventy-five to be exact, including citrus peel, honey, basil, rosemary, and sage. A mere ½ ounce in the drink makes for an aromatic cocktail with a honeyed sweetness. For a refreshing S.S. Manhattan, add 2 ounces fresh orange juice.

Stir the liquid ingredients in a mixing glass with ice. Strain into a chilled cocktail glass. Run the lemon peel around the rim, twist it over the drink, and drop it in.

2½ ounces bourbon
½ ounce Bénédictine
Lemon peel twist

Bent Nail

LIKE MANY WHISKEY-BASED DRINKS, the Bent Nail must be made with the specific whiskey called for—in this case, Canadian blended whisky. This drink is the Canadian take on the Rusty Nail, which is made with blended scotch. There's only a hair-splitting difference between the Bent Nail and the Mammamattawa, which calls for generic cherry brandy instead of fine kirsch, which is a cherry eau-de-vie-style brandy with a slight bitter almond flavor. Now that you're properly confused, shake one up to clear your head.

1½ ounces Canadian
blended whisky
½ ounce Drambuie
¼ ounce kirsch

Shake the ingredients vigorously with ice. Strain into a chilled cocktail glass.

Commonwealth

YOU SIMPLY CANNOT GO WRONG with this classically well-balanced combination of whisky, lemon juice, and orange liqueur. Bourbon lovers may want to try the Chapel Hill, which replaces the Canadian with bourbon and the Grand Marnier with Cointreau. For a potent variation on the Chapel Hill, add 1½ ounces brandy to make a French Twist.

Shake the liquid ingredients vigorously with ice. Strain into a chilled cocktail glass. Twist the orange peel over the drink, and drop it in.

1½ ounces Canadian whisky
½ ounce Grand Marnier
¼ ounce fresh lemon juice
Orange peel twist

Godfather

AMARETTO LENDS A MELLOWING ELEMENT to this popular drink from the 1970s. Although blended scotch is the traditional whiskey used, bourbon is equally tasty.

Shake the ingredients vigorously with ice. Strain into an ice-filled old-fashioned glass.

2 ounces blended scotch
  or bourbon
1 ounce amaretto

Scotch Mist

TO OBTAIN THE IDEAL "MIST," you must pack a chilled glass with crushed ice to get that dramatic Scottish-precipitation effect once the spirit is poured into the glass. This drink should be sipped appreciatively using a good-quality single-malt scotch.

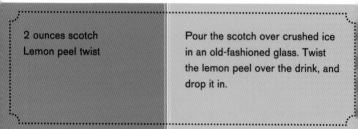

2 ounces scotch
Lemon peel twist

Pour the scotch over crushed ice in an old-fashioned glass. Twist the lemon peel over the drink, and drop it in.

Seven and Seven

A NO-BRAINER, with a title that makes it real easy to remember the ingredients—but sooo smooth, you might just forget how many you've had.

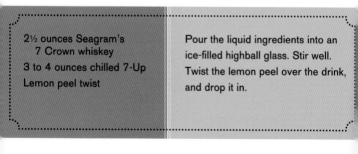

2½ ounces Seagram's 7 Crown whiskey
3 to 4 ounces chilled 7-Up
Lemon peel twist

Pour the liquid ingredients into an ice-filled highball glass. Stir well. Twist the lemon peel over the drink, and drop it in.

Bourbon Buck

BUCKS ARE TRADITIONALLY MADE WITH GIN, but this drink takes the Southern route, becoming the perfect late-afternoon-on-the-veranda quencher. It's also customary to drop the citrus wedge, once it has been squeezed, into the glass.

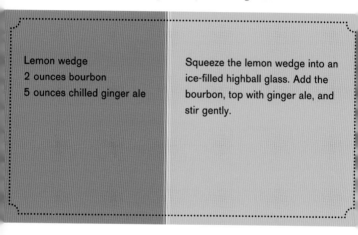

Lemon wedge
2 ounces bourbon
5 ounces chilled ginger ale

Squeeze the lemon wedge into an ice-filled highball glass. Add the bourbon, top with ginger ale, and stir gently.

· Variations · For a SCOTCH BUCK, substitute scotch for the bourbon.

For an IRISH BUCK, substitute Irish whiskey for the bourbon.

For a HORSE'S NECK, add a dash of Angostura bitters, and coil a lemon peel spiral in the highball glass.

For a PRESBYTERIAN, reduce the ginger ale to 2 ounces, add 2 ounces club soda, and garnish with a lemon twist, omitting the lemon wedge.

Mississippi Mist

WHAT COULD BE MORE COPACETIC than a cocktail that partners bourbon with Southern Comfort, a peach-flavored bourbon-based liqueur with roots in New Orleans? Pure Southern charm misting in a glass.

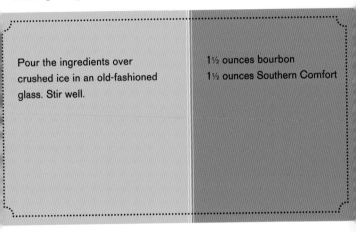

Pour the ingredients over crushed ice in an old-fashioned glass. Stir well.

1½ ounces bourbon
1½ ounces Southern Comfort

· Variations · For a KENTUCKY COWHAND, add ¼ ounce light cream. Shake and serve up.

For a LITTLE COLONEL, add 1 ounce fresh lime juice. Shake and serve up.

savvy

· Essential recipes for every bartender ·

Alabama Slammer

SOUTHERN COMFORT, WITH ITS PEACH FLAVOR, has an enticing way of adding fruity notes to a cocktail, and with the flavors of almond, sloeberry, and orange, the resulting drink becomes absolutely delectable.

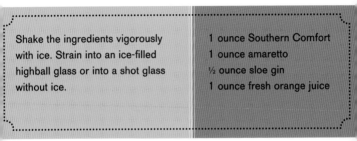

Shake the ingredients vigorously with ice. Strain into an ice-filled highball glass or into a shot glass without ice.

1 ounce Southern Comfort
1 ounce amaretto
½ ounce sloe gin
1 ounce fresh orange juice

Boilermaker

YES, THIS IS THE CLASSIC WHISKEY SHOT WITH A BEER CHASER, and if you must draw attention to yourself, the ritual of dropping the shot glass into the mug of beer is quite effective.

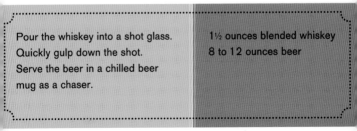

Pour the whiskey into a shot glass. Quickly gulp down the shot. Serve the beer in a chilled beer mug as a chaser.

1½ ounces blended whiskey
8 to 12 ounces beer

Rob Roy

THE NAME MAY HAVE A SWASHBUCKLING LINEAGE, in honor of the legendary seventeenth-century Scottish brigand Robert MacGregor (hero of Sir Walter Scott's novel from the 1800s), but it's probably just a thinly veiled excuse to use scotch instead of rye or bourbon in a Manhattan.

2½ ounces blended scotch
½ ounce sweet vermouth
Dash of Angostura bitters
Maraschino cherry

Stir the liquid ingredients in a mixing glass with ice. Strain into a chilled cocktail glass or into an ice-filled old-fashioned glass. Garnish with the cherry.

· Variations · For a DRY ROB ROY, substitute dry vermouth for the sweet vermouth, and garnish with a lemon peel twist.

For a PERFECT ROB ROY, use ¼ ounce dry vermouth and ¼ ounce sweet vermouth, and garnish with a lemon peel twist.

For a CHANCELLOR, replace the sweet vermouth with dry, and add 1 ounce of ruby port.

John Collins

A VARIATION ON THE GIN-BASED TOM COLLINS, the John Collins is made with either bourbon or Canadian blended whisky. To confuse matters, sometimes the Canadian whisky version is called a Captain Collins, while the bourbon-based drink is also known as a Colonel Collins and even a Bourbon Collins.

Shake the bourbon, lemon juice, and simple syrup vigorously with ice. Strain into an ice-filled collins glass. Top with club soda, and stir gently. Garnish with the lemon, orange, and cherry.

2 ounces bourbon or blended Canadian whisky

1 ounce fresh lemon juice

½ ounce simple syrup or 1 teaspoon superfine sugar

5 to 6 ounces club soda

Lemon and orange slices

Maraschino cherry

· Basic Simple Syrup · Also known as SUGAR SYRUP, this is an essential ingredient in many drinks, as it requires no dissolving or excessive stirring to incorporate, unlike granulated sugar. Makes 2 cups.

1 cup water   2 cups sugar

In a small saucepan, bring the water to a boil. Remove the pan from the heat and add the sugar. Stir until the sugar is completely dissolved. Cool completely before using or refrigerating. Pour into a clean glass jar, cap tightly, and store (indefinitely) in the refrigerator until needed.

Classic Manhattan

THIS CLASSIC AMERICAN APERITIF beautifully combines whiskey, vermouth, and bitters, which come together for optimum smoothness. The type of whiskey used is a crucial element. A classic Manhattan traditionally must be made with rye. However, the harsher bite of rye has fallen out of favor, and many Americans prefer the sweetness of bourbon. Blended Canadian whisky comes close to rye, yet makes a mellower Manhattan. Whichever way you swing, a premium whiskey will always give the best results. The drink is classically served up in a cocktail glass, but many prefer it over ice in an old-fashioned glass, which gives it a bit of dilution and chill. Variations include using 1 ounce of sweet vermouth for a Sweet Manhattan or for a Dry Manhattan using ¾ ounce dry vermouth in place of the sweet (which is somewhat oxymoronic, as the quintessential Manhattan is by definition a sweet vermouth–based drink). Both variations call for a lemon peel twist.

Stir the liquid ingredients in a mixing glass with ice. Strain into a chilled cocktail glass. Garnish with the cherry.

2 ounces rye, bourbon, or blended Canadian whisky

¾ ounce sweet vermouth

2 to 3 dashes Angostura bitters

Maraschino cherry

Perfect Manhattan

PERFECT IN COCKTAIL TERMS always connotes half sweet and half dry vermouth.

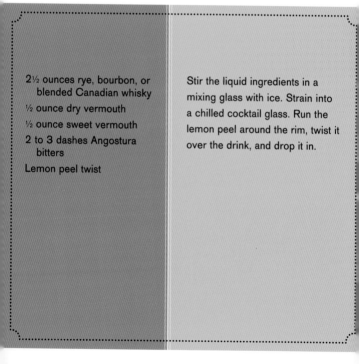

2½ ounces rye, bourbon, or blended Canadian whisky
½ ounce dry vermouth
½ ounce sweet vermouth
2 to 3 dashes Angostura bitters
Lemon peel twist

Stir the liquid ingredients in a mixing glass with ice. Strain into a chilled cocktail glass. Run the lemon peel around the rim, twist it over the drink, and drop it in.

Bourbon Sling

A SLING, BY ITS VERY NATURE, IS A CITRUS-BASED BUBBLY AFFAIR, and this one is no exception. Although slings are typically sweetened with a fruit brandy, the Bourbon Sling takes a decidedly Southern approach, using Southern Comfort instead, and a lemon wedge fills in for the traditional lime peel twist.

Shake the liquid ingredients except the club soda vigorously with ice. Strain into an ice-filled highball glass. Top with club soda and stir gently. Squeeze the lemon wedge over the drink, and drop it in.

2½ ounces bourbon
½ ounce Southern Comfort
½ ounce fresh lemon juice
5 to 6 ounces chilled club soda
Lemon wedge

Traditional Southern-Style Mint Julep

SYNONYMOUS WITH THE KENTUCKY DERBY, which is held on the first Saturday in May, this Southern drink has been around since the late 1800s. Essential to a sublime julep is a fine Kentucky bourbon of the premium single-batch variety. The classic silver julep cup achieves its dramatic signature frost from condensation as the bourbon and crushed ice are stirred—but it's perfectly acceptable to serve a Mint Julep in a collins, highball, or old-fashioned glass.

Originally, the mint sprig was simply an aromatic flourish at the edge of the drink, extended above the rim to allow one to inhale its aroma while sipping the bourbon. However, some insist on muddling the mint first to infuse the bourbon with its fragrant intensity, so I've included the muddled version as well (see page 34).

4 ounces Kentucky bourbon

½ ounce simple syrup (page 27) or 1 teaspoon superfine sugar

4 to 6 fresh mint sprigs

Pour the liquid ingredients into a julep cup or collins glass filled with crushed ice. Stir well until the glass is frosty. Garnish with the mint sprigs, extending them above the rim, and serve with a straw.

Muddled Mint Julep

THE TREATMENT OF THE MINT is still a hotly debated subject among southerners, so to keep things copacetic, here is the mint-lover's version. An additional splash of club soda or water makes a refreshingly tall highball.

12 to 14 fresh mint leaves

½ ounce simple syrup (page 27) or 1 teaspoon superfine sugar

4 ounces Kentucky bourbon

2 to 3 fresh mint sprigs

Lemon peel twist (optional)

Muddle the mint leaves and simple syrup in the bottom of a chilled julep cup or old-fashioned glass. Fill the glass with crushed ice, add the bourbon, and stir until the glass is frosty. Garnish with more mint sprigs, extending them above the rim, and add a twist of lemon peel, if desired.

Rusty Nail

FANTASTICALLY POPULAR WITH THE 1960s SWINGING SET, this drink has stood the test of time. If it's too sweet for your taste, make a drier version by using only ¼ ounce of Drambuie, and if you want a few citrus and herbal notes, add ½ ounce Lillet Blanc. For a Prince Edward, simply garnish with an orange slice.

Pour the liquid ingredients into an ice-filled highball glass. Stir well. Twist the lemon peel over the drink, and drop it in.

1½ ounces scotch
1 ounce Drambuie
Lemon peel twist

Old-Fashioned

AS WITH MOST COCKTAILS THAT HAVE BEEN AROUND FOREVER, the original components of this classic American drink have been tweaked and embellished. Concocted at the Pendennis Club of Louisville, Kentucky, in the late 1800s, the type of whiskey used has gone through many transmutations. Kentucky bourbon is a popular choice, but some prefer rye, and smooth blended whiskey has its fans as well. The drink even inspired a sturdy, heavy-bottomed glass of the same name, which was specifically designed to accommodate the muddling of those supplemental fruits with the sugar and bitters. The resulting juices produce the familiar Old-Fashioned flavor many revere.

1 sugar cube or 1 teaspoon sugar

3 dashes Angostura bitters

1 strip lemon zest

1 orange slice

1 maraschino cherry

2½ ounces bourbon or blended whiskey

2 to 3 ounces chilled club soda (optional)

Orange slice

Maraschino cherry

In the bottom of a chilled old-fashioned glass, saturate the sugar cube with the bitters. Add lemon zest, orange slice, and cherry. Muddle together the sugar, bitters, and fruit. Fill the glass with ice, add the whiskey, and stir well. Top with club soda, if desired. Garnish with the orange slice and cherry.

· Variations · For an ECCENTRIC OLD-FASHIONED, place 1 complete lemon peel spiral in the glass. Shake 2 ounces blended whiskey, a dash of curaçao, and ½ teaspoon sugar, and strain into the glass.

For a SCOTCH OLD-FASHIONED, substitute blended scotch for the bourbon.

For the fruitier CLAREMONT, muddle 2 maraschino cherries and 2 orange slices, and add ¾ ounce orange curaçao.

Sazerac

THIS NEW ORLEANS CLASSIC was the first drink to be specifically called a "cocktail." In the 1830s, a French pharmacist named Peychaud—yes, the bitters guy—began serving up this soothing elixir made with the French Cognac Sazerac de Forge et Fils and his eponymous bitters for, um, digestive unrest. Later versions opted for cheaper American rye instead of Cognac, and anise-flavored absinthe was introduced into the alchemy and later replaced with Pernod once absinthe became illegal. These days, a great bourbon or rye is often preferred, and in New Orleans, the locals favor Herbsaint over Pernod.

The glass for a Sazerac must be thoroughly chilled, and although purists will tell you not to drop the lemon peel twist in the drink, a subtle spritz of lemon oil is quite pleasant. For a New Orleans Sazerac (also called a New Orleans Cocktail), add ½ ounce fresh lemon juice and Herbsaint. Later recipes have added a sugar cube and water to the original.

Coat the inside of a chilled old-fashioned glass with the Pernod, discarding the excess. Shake the bourbon and bitters with ice. Strain into the prepared glass. Twist the lemon peel over the drink, and drop it in.

- 1 teaspoon Pernod or Herbsaint
- 2 ounces bourbon or rye whiskey
- 3 to 4 dashes Peychaud's bitters
- Lemon peel twist

Wally Wallbanger

HARVEY HAS MOVED FROM THE WEST COAST, affected a Southern drawl, and joined the good ol' boys club with this bourbon-lemon-mint variation on the vodka-based Wallbanger, complete with a splash of licorice-flavored Galliano to add a Continental note.

1½ ounces bourbon
½ ounce Galliano
1 ounce fresh lemon juice
1 teaspoon sugar
Fresh mint sprig

Shake the liquid ingredients and sugar vigorously with ice. Strain into an ice-filled old-fashioned glass. Garnish with the mint sprig.

Whiskey Rickey

THE WHISKEY RICKEY IS SIMILAR TO A COLLINS OR FIZZ, but its defining characteristic is the refreshingly tart omission of sugar. This combo is so versatile that the type of whiskey used is entirely up to you.

Shake the whiskey and lime juice vigorously with ice. Strain into an ice-filled highball glass. Top with club soda, and stir gently. Squeeze the lime wedge over the drink, and drop it in.

2 ounces bourbon, blended scotch, Irish, or blended whiskey

½ ounce fresh lime juice

3 to 5 ounces chilled club soda

Lime wedge

Whiskey Sour

THE KING OF ALL SOURS, this refreshing drink was perfectly described in *Esquire's 1945 Handbook for Hosts*: "This is simply a species of fortified lemonade in concentrated form." Key to a sublime Whiskey Sour is freshly squeezed lemon juice. Although many prefer the drink with bourbon, a blended whiskey or other favorite whiskey is perfectly acceptable. Always shaken and traditionally served in a sour glass, it can also be served up or in a highball glass with ice.

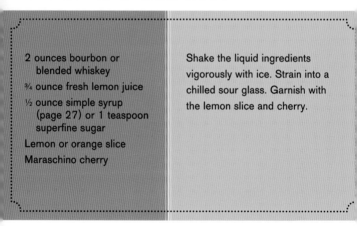

2 ounces bourbon or
   blended whiskey
¾ ounce fresh lemon juice
½ ounce simple syrup
   (page 27) or 1 teaspoon
   superfine sugar
Lemon or orange slice
Maraschino cherry

Shake the liquid ingredients vigorously with ice. Strain into a chilled sour glass. Garnish with the lemon slice and cherry.

· Variations · For a FRISCO SOUR, add ¼ ounce Bénédictine and ½ ounce fresh lime juice.

For a NEW YORK SOUR, float ½ ounce dry red wine on top of a Whiskey Sour. Garnish with a lemon slice.

· sophisticated ·

· A little more work but definitely worth the effort ·

New Yorker

AN OLD-FASHIONED DONE NEW YORK STYLE, with a zing of lime and a fussy dash of grenadine. A slight variant is the New York Cocktail, which replaces the bourbon with blended whiskey. For a yummy after-dinner drink, the Commodore adds 1 ounce crème de cacao and switches out the lime for lemon juice.

Pour the bourbon and lime juice into an ice-filled old-fashioned glass. Add the grenadine and sugar, and stir well. Twist the lemon and orange peels over the drink, and drop them in.

1½ ounces bourbon or rye
¾ ounce fresh lime juice
Dash of grenadine
1 teaspoon sugar
Lemon and orange peel twists

Belmont Breeze

SURE TO BECOME A CLASSIC, the Belmont Breeze is the new official drink of the Belmont Stakes. It was created by Dale DeGroff, master mixologist from New York City.

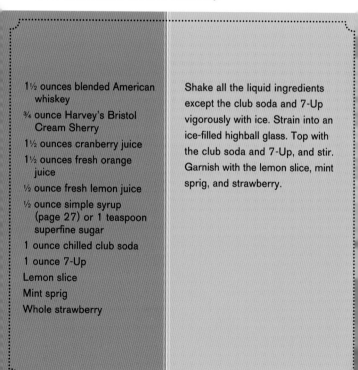

1½ ounces blended American whiskey

¾ ounce Harvey's Bristol Cream Sherry

1½ ounces cranberry juice

1½ ounces fresh orange juice

½ ounce fresh lemon juice

½ ounce simple syrup (page 27) or 1 teaspoon superfine sugar

1 ounce chilled club soda

1 ounce 7-Up

Lemon slice

Mint sprig

Whole strawberry

Shake all the liquid ingredients except the club soda and 7-Up vigorously with ice. Strain into an ice-filled highball glass. Top with the club soda and 7-Up, and stir. Garnish with the lemon slice, mint sprig, and strawberry.

Nevins

INFUSE BOURBON with an abundance of tart citrus and fruity brandy, and you get this little gem of a cocktail.

Shake the ingredients vigorously with ice. Strain into a chilled cocktail glass.

1½ ounces bourbon
½ ounce apricot brandy
Dash of Angostura bitters
1 ounce fresh grapefruit juice
½ ounce fresh lemon juice

Scarlett O'Hara

A LITTLE TARTY AND FULL OF SASS, this delicious New Orleans classic is named after the quintessential Southern belle.

Shake the ingredients vigorously with ice. Strain into a chilled cocktail glass.

2 ounces Southern Comfort
2 ounces cranberry juice
½ ounce fresh lemon juice
½ ounce fresh lime juice
1 teaspoon sugar

Bobby Burns

A VARIATION ON THE ROB ROY, this Scottish classic has a decidedly herbal note from Bénédictine and is named after the poet who wrote "Auld Lang Syne" and "Coming Through the Rye." For those who prefer Irish whiskey (we won't tell), try the Brainstorm, made with ¼ ounce dry vermouth instead of the sweet and a twist of orange peel instead of lemon.

1½ ounces blended scotch whisky
1½ ounces sweet vermouth
¼ ounce Bénédictine
Lemon peel twist

Shake the liquid ingredients vigorously with ice. Strain into a chilled cocktail glass. Twist the lemon peel over the drink, and drop it in.

Canadian Cocktail

A MELLOW COCKTAIL, laced with orange liqueur, that is custom-made for Canadian whisky aficionados.

Shake the ingredients vigorously with ice. Strain into an ice-filled old-fashioned glass or into a chilled cocktail glass.

2 ounces Canadian blended whisky

½ ounce Cointreau

2 dashes Angostura bitters

½ ounce simple syrup (page 27) or 1 teaspoon superfine sugar

Derby

DESPITE THE NAME, this cocktail has quite the sunny disposition, courtesy of zingy lime juice, orange liqueur, and aromatic mint.

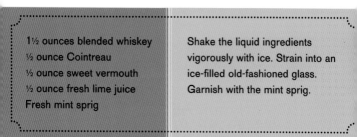

1½ ounces blended whiskey
½ ounce Cointreau
½ ounce sweet vermouth
½ ounce fresh lime juice
Fresh mint sprig

Shake the liquid ingredients vigorously with ice. Strain into an ice-filled old-fashioned glass. Garnish with the mint sprig.

Waldorf Cocktail

THE BARTENDERS AT NEW YORK'S FAMOUS WALDORF ASTORIA added sweet vermouth to this variation on the Sazerac.

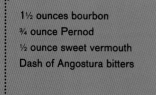

1½ ounces bourbon
¾ ounce Pernod
½ ounce sweet vermouth
Dash of Angostura bitters

Stir the ingredients in a mixing glass with ice. Strain into a chilled cocktail glass.

Ward Eight

THIS CLASSIC FROM BOSTON is named after an election district, but that's not the exciting part—what you should really be jazzed about is that this elaboration on the Whiskey Sour gets more votes for tastiness.

Shake the liquid ingredients vigorously with ice. Strain into an ice-filled old-fashioned glass or a chilled cocktail glass. Garnish with the lemon, orange, and cherry.

2 ounces bourbon or rye
Dash of grenadine
1 ounce fresh lemon juice
1 ounce fresh orange juice
Lemon and orange slices
Maraschino cherry

Irish Shillelagh

THIS POTENT, FRUITY DRINK is named for the Irish policemen's nightstick, for obvious reason—a few of these and you'll start seeing stars.

1½ ounces Irish whiskey
½ ounce light rum
½ ounce sloe gin
1 ounce fresh lemon juice
1 teaspoon sugar
Peach slice
Orange slice
2 to 3 raspberries
Maraschino cherry

Shake the liquid ingredients and sugar vigorously with ice. Strain into an ice-filled old-fashioned glass. Garnish with the fruit.

Kentucky Sidecar

A FEW YEARS BACK, AROUND KENTUCKY DERBY TIME, my cohorts in revelry were clamoring for something "julepy" yet modern. Given my love for a good Sidecar, I came up with this refreshing hybrid, which decadently melds the best of both. I found that a good-quality small-batch bourbon gives the drink a luxurious complexity.

Rub the rim of a chilled cocktail glass with the lemon wedge, and rim with sugar. Shake the liquid ingredients vigorously with ice. Strain into the prepared glass. Garnish with the mint sprig and lemon slice, if desired.

Lemon or tangerine wedge
Sugar
1½ ounces small-batch bourbon
¾ ounce Cointreau
1 ounce fresh tangerine juice
½ ounce fresh lemon juice
1 tall, lush fresh mint sprig
Lemon slice (optional)

· Variations · For a super minty version, add 4 or 5 fresh mint leaves to the cocktail shaker, and shake with the liquid ingredients.

For a KENTUCKY FIZZ, serve over ice in an old-fashioned glass with a splash of club soda.

For a KENTUCKY ORANGE BLOSSOM, increase the tangerine juice to 1½ ounces. Omit the lemon juice. Add a dash of orange flower water, and serve over ice in an old-fashioned glass.

Blarney Stone

ASSERTIVE ANISE-FLAVORED PERNOD gives Irish whiskey a complex edge and the imbiber a smooth tongue.

2 ounces Irish whiskey
¼ ounce Cointreau
¼ ounce Pernod or anisette
Dash of maraschino liqueur
Dash of Angostura bitters
Lemon peel twist

Stir the liquid ingredients in a mixing glass with ice. Strain into a chilled cocktail glass. Run the lemon peel around the rim, twist it over the drink, and drop it in.

Vieux Carré

THIS CLASSIC NEW ORLEANS COCKTAIL hails from the French Quarter. Concocted in the 1930s as the signature drink of the Carousel Bar at the Monteleone Hotel, the Vieux Carré has a perfect balance of favorite flavors the city is famous for.

Shake the liquid ingredients vigorously with ice. Strain into an ice-filled old-fashioned glass. Garnish with the lemon twist.

½ ounce rye whiskey
½ ounce Cognac
½ ounce sweet vermouth
½ teaspoon Bénédictine
Dash of Peychaud's bitters
Dash of Angostura bitters
Lemon peel twist

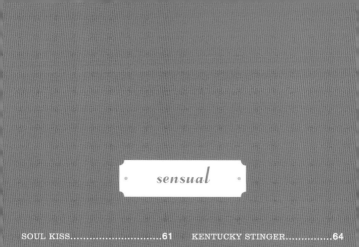

sensual

· Luxurious yumminess for your mouth ·

Soul Kiss

DUBONNET WAS THE 1970S' SEXY LIBATION FOR LOVE, so it's no surprise to find it slipped into this classic cocktail. The French version of the Soul Kiss, the Rue de Rivoli, is made with 1 ounce of each liquor and served over ice in an old-fashioned glass.

Shake the ingredients vigorously with ice. Strain into a chilled cocktail glass.

2 ounces blended Canadian whisky or bourbon

¼ ounce dry vermouth

¼ ounce Dubonnet Rouge

½ ounce fresh orange juice

Louisville Stinger

LIKE A TRUE STINGER, this cocktail has all the rich, heady elements of a great after-dinner tipple.

Shake the ingredients vigorously with ice. Strain into a chilled cocktail glass.

1 ounce bourbon

1 ounce light rum

½ ounce white crème de cacao

¼ ounce white crème de menthe

Bourbon Milk Punch

NEW ORLEANS'S FAVORITE RIFF on the classic rum-based Milk Punch pushes the cocktail into the after-dinner realm with the additional lusciousness of crème de cacao, vanilla, and spices.

Shake the liquid ingredients and cinnamon vigorously with ice. Strain into an ice-filled old-fashioned glass. Sprinkle the top with nutmeg.

2 ounces bourbon

½ ounce dark crème de cacao

4 ounces milk or 3 ounces half-and-half

Dash of vanilla extract

¼ teaspoon ground cinnamon

Freshly grated or ground nutmeg

Kentucky Stinger

THE STINGER HAS COME A LONG WAY FROM PROHIBITION DAYS, when crème de menthe was an effective mask not only for subpar liquor but also 100-proof breath. This rendition heads south, with a sweet and fruity splash of Southern Comfort.

1½ ounces bourbon
¼ ounce Southern Comfort
¼ ounce white crème
  de menthe

Shake the ingredients vigorously with ice. Strain into an ice-filled wineglass.

Everybody's Irish

LOOKING FOR SOMETHING A BIT MORE NOVEL for the next St. Pat's holiday? I'm not quite sure what the Carthusian monks who created Chartreuse would make of this drink, but it definitely fills the color criteria and adds a welcoming herbal note to the predictable crème de menthe.

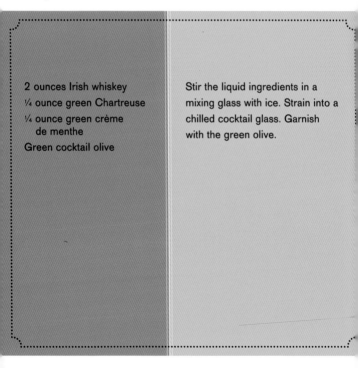

2 ounces Irish whiskey
¼ ounce green Chartreuse
¼ ounce green crème de menthe
Green cocktail olive

Stir the liquid ingredients in a mixing glass with ice. Strain into a chilled cocktail glass. Garnish with the green olive.

Shamrock

YES, ANOTHER ST. PAT'S DAY LIBATION—but in the Shamrock, cream adds a lush, velvety texture, most soothing after a night of green-tinged festivities. For a frosty treat, add 4 ounces vanilla ice cream, combine in a blender until smooth, and serve in a chilled wineglass.

Shake the liquid ingredients vigorously with ice. Strain into an ice-filled old-fashioned glass. Garnish with the cherry.

1½ ounces Irish whiskey
¾ ounce green crème de menthe
2 ounces heavy cream
Maraschino cherry

· *stimulating* ·

· Caffeinated and fizzy drinks for a fun buzz ·

Whiskey Fizz

AKIN TO THE WHISKEY SOUR, this drink is that much more refreshing due to the addition of carbonation. For a Waterloo, add ¾ ounce Mandarine Napoléon liqueur (of course) and replace the garnish with an orange slice.

Shake the whiskey, lemon juice, and simple syrup vigorously with ice. Strain into an ice-filled highball glass. Top with club soda, and stir gently. Squeeze the lemon wedge over the drink, and drop it in.

2 ounces blended or other whiskey

1 ounce fresh lemon juice

½ ounce simple syrup (page 27) or 1 teaspoon superfine sugar

3 to 5 ounces chilled club soda

Lemon wedge

Bourbon Swizzle

SWIZZLES ORIGINATED IN THE CARIBBEAN, where they were named after the "swizzle stick," a twig used to agitate tall rum drinks. In this case, a jazz musician's drumstick may be more appropriate.

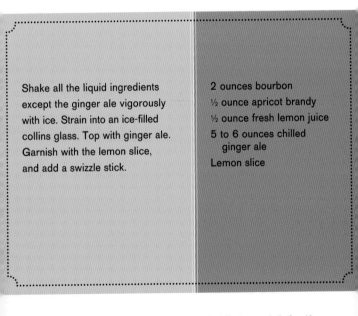

Shake all the liquid ingredients except the ginger ale vigorously with ice. Strain into an ice-filled collins glass. Top with ginger ale. Garnish with the lemon slice, and add a swizzle stick.

2 ounces bourbon
½ ounce apricot brandy
½ ounce fresh lemon juice
5 to 6 ounces chilled
  ginger ale
Lemon slice

· Variations · For a SCOTCH SWIZZLE, substitute scotch for the bourbon, triple sec for the apricot brandy, and lime juice for the lemon juice.

Churchill Downs Cooler

EFFERVESCENTLY REFRESHING AND POTENT, this cooler is sure to fuel a day of wagering at the races.

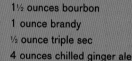

1½ ounces bourbon
1 ounce brandy
½ ounce triple sec
4 ounces chilled ginger ale

Pour all ingredients but the ginger ale into an ice-filled highball glass. Top with the ginger ale, and stir gently.

Mamie Taylor

A CENTURY AFTER THE CREATION OF THIS DRINK, we still don't know who the mysterious Ms. Taylor is or why a drink was named after her. Nonetheless, if you're looking for a great cocktail to enjoy with blended scotch, try this delightfully refreshing highball.

Pour the scotch and lime juice into an ice-filled highball glass. Top with ginger ale and stir gently. Garnish with the lemon slice.

2 ounces blended scotch
½ ounce fresh lime juice
3 to 5 ounces chilled ginger ale
Lemon slice

Iced Irish Coffee

LIFE WILL BE GOOD WHEN STARBUCKS STARTS SERVING THESE—all the stimulating elements of the classic Irish Coffee translate nicely from hot to cold.

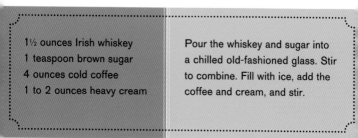

1½ ounces Irish whiskey
1 teaspoon brown sugar
4 ounces cold coffee
1 to 2 ounces heavy cream

Pour the whiskey and sugar into a chilled old-fashioned glass. Stir to combine. Fill with ice, add the coffee and cream, and stir.

Mint Condition

AS SMOOTH AS FLOWING LAVA BUT AS VOLATILE AS A VOLCANO, the Mint Condition will spark up any occasion.

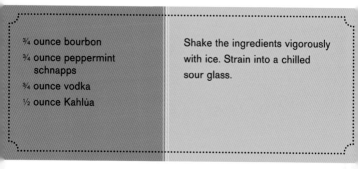

¾ ounce bourbon
¾ ounce peppermint schnapps
¾ ounce vodka
½ ounce Kahlúa

Shake the ingredients vigorously with ice. Strain into a chilled sour glass.

Poire Williams Fizz

THIS DELICIOUSLY FRUITY FIZZ OF A SUMMER DRINK combines the warmth of whiskey with Poire Williams, a pear-flavored brandy-based liqueur, and refreshingly tarts up the combo with citrus.

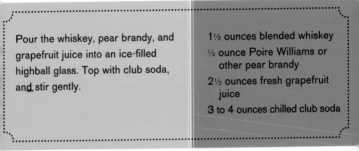

Pour the whiskey, pear brandy, and grapefruit juice into an ice-filled highball glass. Top with club soda, and stir gently.

1½ ounces blended whiskey
½ ounce Poire Williams or other pear brandy
2½ ounces fresh grapefruit juice
3 to 4 ounces chilled club soda

Casanova

A HIGHLY SEDUCTIVE COMBINATION of coffee-flavored Kahlúa and aromatic Marsala add depth to this creamy bourbon cocktail.

Shake the ingredients vigorously with ice. Strain into a chilled cocktail glass.

1½ ounces bourbon
¾ ounce Kahlúa
¾ ounce sweet Marsala
1 ounce heavy cream

Index

Liquid Measurements

BAR SPOON	½ ounce
1 teaspoon	⅙ ounce
1 tablespoon	½ ounce
2 tablespoons (PONY)	1 ounce
3 tablespoons (JIGGER)	1½ ounces
¼ cup	2 ounces
⅓ cup	3 ounces
½ cup	4 ounces
⅔ cup	5 ounces
¾ cup	6 ounces
1 cup	8 ounces
1 pint	16 ounces
1 quart	32 ounces
750-ml bottle	25.4 ounces
1-liter bottle	33.8 ounces
1 medium lemon	3 tablespoons juice
1 medium lime	2 tablespoons juice
1 medium orange	⅓ cup juice

KENTUCKY COLONEL · BENT NAIL · C

MIST · SEVEN AND SEVEN · BOURBO

SLAMMER · BOILERMAKER · ROB ROY

PERFECT MANHATTAN · BOURBON S

MINT JULEP · MUDDLED MINT JULEP ·

WALLY WALLBANGER · WHISKEY RICKEY

BREEZE · NEVINS · SCARLETT O'HARA

DERBY · WALDORF COCKTAIL · WARD

SIDECAR · BLARNEY STONE · VIEUX C.

BOURBON MILK PUNCH · KENTUCKY ST

WHISKEY FIZZ · BOURBON SWIZZLE · CH

ICED IRISH COFFEE · MINT CONDITI